TEACHINGS OF THE MASTER

TEACHINGS OF THE MASTER

THE COLLECTED SAYINGS OF JESUS CHRIST

COMPILED BY PHILIP LAW

WESTMINSTER JOHN KNOX PRESS
LOUISVILLE, KENTUCKY

Parts 1 and 7: Scripture quotations are from the
New Jerusalem Bible, copyright © 1985 by Darton,
Longman & Todd, Ltd., and Doubleday, a division
of Bantam Doubleday Dell Publishing Group, Inc.
Reprinted by permission of the publishers.

Parts 2 and 6: Scripture quotations are from the New
Revised Standard Version of the Bible are copyright
© 1989 by the Division of Christian Education of the
National Council of the Churches of Christ in the
U.S.A. and are used by permission.

Parts 3 and 5: Scripture quotations are from the Revised
English Bible, © Oxford University Press and
Cambridge University Press, 1989. Used by permission.

Part 4: Scripture quotations are from The Holy Bible,
New International Version. Copyright © 1973, 1978,
1984 International Bible Society. Used by permission
of Zondervan Bible Publishers.

Published in the United States in 2000 by
Westminster John Knox Press
Louisville, Kentucky

This book is printed on acid-free paper that meets
the American National Standards Institute Z39.48
standard. ♾

Printed in Indonesia by APP Printing Ptd. Ltd.

00 01 02 03 04 05 06 07 08 09 -- 10 9 8 7 6 5 4 3 2 1

Library of Congress Cataloging-in-Publication Data
is on file at the Library of Congress.

ISBN 0-664-22282-X

CONTENTS

1 Part One

The Light Revealed 7

2 Part Two

The Master and His Disciples 19

3 Part Three

The Sermon on the Mount 37

4 Part Four

Proverbs and Shorter Sayings 57

5 Part Five

The Major Parables 69

6 Part Six

The Master and His Opponents 93

7 Part Seven

The Darkness Defeated 111

The Light Revealed

THE WORD
BECOMES FLESH

In the beginning
was the Word:
the Word was with God
and the Word was God.
He was with God in the beginning.
Through him all things came into being,
not one thing came into being except through him.
What has come into being in him was life,
life that was the light of men;

and light shines in darkness,
and darkness could not overpower it …
The Word became flesh,
he lived among us,
and we saw his glory,
the glory that he has from the Father
    as only son of the Father,
full of grace and truth.

John 1:1–5, 14

THE WITNESS OF
JOHN THE BAPTIST

A man came, sent by God.
His name was John.
He came as a witness,
to bear witness to the light,
so that everyone might believe through him.
He was not the light,
he was to bear witness to the light…

This was the witness of John, when the
Jews sent to him priests and Levites from
Jerusalem to ask him, 'Who are you?' He
declared… 'I am, as Isaiah prophesied:

A voice of one that cries in the desert:
Prepare a way for the Lord.
Make his paths straight!…

'I baptize with water; but standing among
you – unknown to you – is the one who is
coming after me; and I am not fit to undo
the strap of his sandal.' This happened at
Bethany, on the far side of the Jordan,
where John was baptizing.

John 1:6–8, 19, 20, 23, 26–28

THE MASTER CALLS HIS FIRST DISCIPLES

The next day as John stood there again with two of his disciples, Jesus went past, and John looked towards him and said, 'Look, there is the lamb of God.' And the two disciples heard what he said and followed Jesus. Jesus turned round, saw them following and said, 'What do you want?' They answered, 'Rabbi' – which means Teacher – 'where do you live?' He replied, 'Come and see'; so they went and saw where he lived, and stayed with him that day. It was about the tenth hour.

One of these two who became followers of Jesus after hearing what John had said was Andrew, the brother of Simon Peter. The first thing Andrew did was to find his brother and say to him, 'We have found the Messiah' – which means the Christ – and he took Simon to Jesus.

Jesus looked at him and said, 'You are Simon son of John; you are to be called Cephas' – which means Rock.

John 1:35–42

BORN OF THE SPIRIT

There was one of the Pharisees called Nicodemus, a leader of the Jews, who came to Jesus by night and said, 'Rabbi, we know that you have come from God as a teacher; for no one could perform the signs that you do unless God were with him.' Jesus answered:

In all truth I tell you,
no one can see the kingdom of God
without being born from above.

Nicodemus said, 'How can anyone who is already old be born? Is it possible to go back into the womb again and be born?' Jesus replied:

In all truth I tell you,
no one can enter the kingdom of God
without being born
through water and the Spirit;

what is born of human nature is human;
what is born of the Spirit is spirit.
Do not be surprised when I say:
You must be born from above.
The wind blows where it pleases;
you can hear its sound,
but you cannot tell where it comes from
*   or where it is going.*
So it is with everyone
who is born of the Spirit.

John 3:1–8

SPIRIT AND TRUTH

[Jesus] left Judea and went back to Galilee. He had to pass through Samaria. On the

way he came to the Samaritan town called Sychar near the land that Jacob gave to his son Joseph. Jacob's well was there and Jesus, tired by the journey, sat down by the well. It was about the sixth hour. When a Samaritan woman came to draw water, Jesus said to her, 'Give me something to drink.' His disciples had gone into the town to buy food. The

Samaritan woman said to him, 'You are a Jew. How is it that you ask me, a Samaritan, for something to drink?' – Jews, of course, do not associate with Samaritans…
Jesus replied:

Whoever drinks this water
will be thirsty again;
but no one who drinks the water
that I shall give
will ever be thirsty again:
the water that I shall give
will become a spring of water within,
welling up for eternal life…

'I see you are a prophet, sir,' said the woman. 'Our fathers worshipped on this mountain, though you say that Jerusalem is the place where one ought to worship.' Jesus said:

Believe me, woman, the hour is coming
when you will worship the Father
neither on this mountain
nor in Jerusalem.
You worship what you do not know;
we worship what we do know;

for salvation comes from the Jews.
But the hour is coming –
indeed is already here –
when true worshippers
will worship the Father
in spirit and truth:
that is the kind of worshipper
the Father seeks.
God is spirit,
and those who worship
must worship in spirit and truth.

The woman said to him, 'I know that Messiah – that is, Christ – is coming; and when he comes he will explain everything.' Jesus said, 'That is who I am, I who speak to you.'

John 4:3–9, 13–14, 19–26

THE BREAD OF LIFE

[The Jews] said to him, 'What must we do if we are to carry out God's work?' Jesus gave them this answer, 'This is carrying out God's work: you must believe in the one he has sent.' So they said, 'What sign will you yourself do, the sight of which will make us believe in you? What work will you do? Our fathers ate manna in the desert; as scripture says:

"He gave them bread from heaven to eat.'"
　　Jesus answered them:

In all truth I tell you,
it was not Moses
　　who gave you the bread from heaven,
it is my Father
　　who gives you the bread from heaven,
the true bread;
for the bread of God
is the bread
　　which comes down from heaven
and gives life to the world.

'Sir,' they said, 'give us that bread always.'
Jesus answered them:

I am the bread of life...
Anyone who eats this bread
　　will live for ever;
and the bread that I shall give
is my flesh, for the life of the world.

Then the Jews started arguing among
themselves, 'How can this man give
us his flesh to eat?' Jesus replied to
them:

In all truth I tell you,
if you do not eat
　　the flesh of the Son of man
and drink his blood,
you have no life in you.
Anyone who does eat my flesh
　　and drink my blood
has eternal life,
and I shall raise that person up
　　on the last day.
For my flesh is real food
and my blood is real drink.
Whoever eats my flesh
　　and drinks my blood
lives in me
and I live in that person.

John 6:28–35, 51–56

HYPOCRISY AND LOVE

And Jesus went to the Mount of Olives.

At daybreak he appeared in the Temple again; and as all the people came to him, he sat down and began to teach them.

The scribes and Pharisees brought a woman along who had been caught 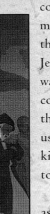 committing adultery; and making her stand there in the middle they said to Jesus, 'Master, this woman was caught in the very act of committing adultery, and in the Law Moses has ordered us to stone women of this kind. What have you got to say?'

They asked him this as a test, looking for an accusation to use against him. But Jesus bent down and started writing on the ground with his finger. As they persisted with their question, he straightened up and said, 'Let the one among you who is guiltless be the first to throw a stone at her.' Then he bent down and continued writing on the ground.

When they heard this they went away one by one, beginning with the eldest, until the last one had gone and Jesus was left alone with the woman, who remained in the middle. Jesus again straightened up and said, 'Woman, where are they? Has no one condemned you?' 'No one, sir,' she replied. 'Neither do I condemn you,' said Jesus. 'Go away, and from this moment sin no more.'

John 8:1–11

TRUTH AND FREEDOM

When Jesus spoke to the people again, he said:

> *I am the light of the world;*
> *anyone who follows me*
>   *will not be walking in the dark,*
> *but will have the light of life…*
> *You are from below;*
> *I am from above.*
> *You are of this world;*
> *I am not of this world…*

As he was saying this, many came to believe in him.

To the Jews who believed in him Jesus said:

If you make my word your home
you will indeed be my disciples;
you will come to know the truth,
and the truth will set you free.

John 8:12, 23, 30–32

THE LIGHT OF THE WORLD

As he went along, he saw a man who had been blind from birth. His disciples asked him, 'Rabbi, who sinned, this man or his parents, that he should have been born blind?' 'Neither he nor his parents sinned,' Jesus answered, 'he was born blind so that the works of God might be revealed in him.

As long as day lasts
we must carry out the work of the one
  who sent me;
the night will soon be here
  when no one can work.
As long as I am in the world
I am the light of the world.'

Having said this, he spat on the ground, made a paste with the spittle, put this over the eyes of the blind man, and said to him, 'Go and wash in the Pool of Siloam' (the name means 'one who has been sent'). So he went off and washed and came back able to see...

It had been a sabbath day when Jesus made the paste and opened the man's eyes, so when the Pharisees asked him how he had gained his sight, he said, 'He put a paste on my eyes, and I washed, and I can see.' Then some of the Pharisees said, 'That man cannot be from God: he does not keep the

sabbath.' Others said, 'How can a sinner produce signs like this?' And there was division among them…

Jesus said:

> It is for judgment
> that I have come into this world,
> so that those without sight may see
> and those with sight may become blind.

Hearing this, some Pharisees who were present said to him, 'So we are blind, are we?' Jesus replied:

> If you were blind,
> you would not be guilty,
> but since you say, 'We can see,'
> your guilt remains.

John 9:1–7, 14–16, 39–41

THE GATE OF THE SHEEPFOLD

'In all truth I tell you, anyone who does not enter the sheepfold through the gate, but climbs in some other way, is a thief and a bandit…'

Jesus told them this parable but they failed to understand what he was saying to them.

So Jesus spoke to them again:

> In all truth I tell you,
> I am the gate of the sheepfold.
> All who have come before me
> are thieves and bandits,
> but the sheep took no notice of them.
> I am the gate.
> Anyone who enters through me
>   will be safe:
> such a one will go in and out
> and will find pasture.
> The thief comes
>   only to steal and kill and destroy.
>   I have come
>   so that they may have life
>   and have it to the full.

John 10:1, 6–10

THE GOOD SHEPHERD

'I am the good shepherd:
the good shepherd lays down his life
    for his sheep...
I know my own
and my own know me,
just as the Father knows me
and I know the Father;
and I lay down my life for my sheep.

And there are other sheep I have
that are not of this fold,
and I must lead these too.
They too will listen to my voice,
and there will be only one flock,
one shepherd...
The sheep that belong to me
    listen to my voice;

I know them and they follow me.
I give them eternal life;
they will never be lost
and no one will ever steal them
  from my hand.
The Father, for what he has given me,
  is greater than anyone,
and no one can steal anything
  from the Father's hand.
The Father and I are one.'

John 10:11, 14–16, 27–30

Part Two

The Master and His Disciples

THE TWELVE DISCIPLES

Then Jesus summoned his twelve disciples and gave them authority over unclean spirits, to cast them out, and to cure every disease and every sickness. These are the names of the twelve apostles: first, Simon, also known as Peter, and his brother Andrew; James son of Zebedee, and his brother John; Philip and Bartholomew; Thomas and Matthew the tax-collector; James son of Alpheus, and Thaddeus; Simon the Cananean, and Judas Iscariot, the one who betrayed him.

These twelve Jesus sent out with the following instructions...

'See, I am sending you out like sheep into the midst of wolves; so be wise as serpents and innocent as doves.'

Matthew 10:1–5, 16

Fear God, not Man

'A disciple is not above the
teacher, nor a slave above
the master; it is enough for
the disciple to be like the
teacher, and the slave like
the master. If they have
called the master of the
house Beelzebul, how much
more will they malign those
of his household!

'So have no fear of
them; for nothing is
covered up that will not
be uncovered, and nothing
secret that will not become
known. What I say to you
in the dark, tell in the
light; and what you hear
whispered, proclaim from
the housetops. Do not fear
those who kill the body but
cannot kill the soul; rather
fear him who can destroy
both soul and body in hell.
Are not two sparrows sold
for a penny? Yet not one of

them will fall to the ground unperceived by your Father. And even the hairs of your head are all counted. So do not be afraid; you are of more value than many sparrows.'

Matthew 10:24–31

THE COST OF DISCIPLESHIP

'Do not think that I have come to bring peace to the earth; I have not come to bring peace, but a sword.

> For I have come to set a
> man against
> his father,
> and a daughter against
> her mother,
> and a daughter-in-law against
> her mother-in-law;
> and one's foes will be members of
> one's own household.

Whoever loves father or mother more than me is not worthy of me; and whoever loves son or daughter more than me is not worthy of me; and whoever does not take up the cross and follow me is not worthy of me. Those who find their life will lose it, and those who lose their life for my sake will find it.

'Whoever welcomes you welcomes me, and whoever welcomes me welcomes the one who sent me. Whoever welcomes a prophet in the name of a prophet will receive a prophet's reward; and whoever welcomes a righteous person in the name of a righteous person will receive the reward of the righteous; and whoever gives even a cup of cold water to one of these little ones in the name of a disciple – truly I tell you, none of these will lose their reward.'

Matthew 10:34–42

THE KEYS OF THE KINGDOM

Now when Jesus came into the district of Caesarea Philippi, he asked his disciples,

'Who do people say that the Son of man is?'
And they said, 'Some say John the Baptist,
but others Elijah, and still others Jeremiah
or one of the prophets.' He said to them,
'But who do you say that I am?' Simon Peter
answered, 'You are the Messiah, the
Son of the living God.' And Jesus
answered him, 'Blessed are you,
Simon son of Jonah! For flesh and
blood has not revealed this to you,
but my Father in heaven. And I tell
you, you are Peter, and on this rock
I will build my church, and the
gates of Hades will not prevail
against it. I will give you the keys
of the kingdom of heaven, and
whatever you bind on earth will be
bound in heaven, and whatever you
loose on earth will be loosed in
heaven.' Then he sternly ordered
the disciples not to tell anyone
that he was the Messiah.

Matthew 16:13–20

SAVING AND LOSING

Then Jesus told his disciples, 'If any want
to become my followers, let them deny
themselves and take up their cross and
follow me. For those who want to save their
life will lose it, and those who lose their life
for my sake will find it. For what
will it profit them if they gain the
whole world but forfeit their life?
Or what will they give in return
for their life?

'For the Son of man is to
come with his angels in the glory
of his Father, and then he will
repay everyone for what has
been done.'

Matthew 16:24–27

CHILDREN OF GOD

People were bringing little children to him in order that he might touch them; and the disciples spoke sternly to them. But when Jesus saw this, he was indignant and said to them, 'Let the little children come to me; do not stop them; for it is to such as these that the kingdom of God belongs. Truly I tell you, whoever does not receive the kingdom of God as a little child will never enter it.' And he took them up in his arms, laid his hands on them, and blessed them.

Mark 10:13–16

GREATNESS AND HUMILITY

At that time the disciples came to Jesus and asked, 'Who is the greatest in the kingdom of heaven?' He called a child, whom he put among them, and said, 'Truly I tell you, unless you change and become like children, you will never enter the kingdom of heaven. Whoever becomes humble like this child is the greatest in the kingdom of heaven. Whoever welcomes one such child in my name welcomes me.

'If any of you put a stumbling-block before one of these little ones who believe in me, it would be better for you if a great millstone were fastened around your neck and you were drowned in the depth of the sea. Woe to the world because of stumbling-blocks! Occasions for stumbling are bound to come, but woe to the one by whom the stumbling-block comes!...

'Take care that you do not despise one of these little ones; for, I tell you, in heaven their angels continually see the face of my Father in heaven.'

Matthew 18:1–7, 10

BINDING AND LOOSING

'Truly I tell you, whatever you bind on earth will be bound in heaven, and whatever you loose on earth will be loosed in heaven. Again, truly I tell you, if two of you agree on earth about anything you ask, it will be done for you by my Father in heaven. For where two or three are gathered in my name, I am there among them.'

Matthew 18:18–20

LASTING FORGIVENESS

Then Peter came and said to him, 'Lord, if another member of the church sins against me, how often should I forgive? As many as seven times?' Jesus said to him, 'Not seven times, but, I tell you, seventy-seven times.'

Matthew 18:21–22

Eunuchs for the Kingdom of Heaven

'And I say to you, whoever
divorces his wife, except for
unchastity, and marries
another commits adultery.'

   His disciples said to him,
'If such is the case of a man
with his wife, it is better not
to marry.' But he said to
them, 'Not everyone can accept this
teaching, but only those to whom it is given.
For there are eunuchs who have been so from
birth, and there are eunuchs who have been
made eunuchs by others, and there are
eunuchs who have made themselves eunuchs
for the sake of the kingdom of heaven. Let
anyone accept this who can.'

   Matthew 19:9–12

Treasure in Heaven

As he was setting out on a journey, a man
ran up and knelt before him, and asked him,
'Good Teacher, what must I do to inherit
eternal life?' Jesus said to him, 'Why do
you call me good? No one is good but God
alone. You know the commandments:
"You shall not murder; You shall not commit
adultery; You shall not steal; You shall not
bear false witness; You shall not defraud;
Honour your father and mother."' He said
to him, 'Teacher, I have kept all these since
my youth.' Jesus, looking at him, loved him
and said, 'You lack one thing; go, sell what
you own, and give the money to the poor,
and you will have treasure in heaven; then

come, follow me.' When he heard this, he was shocked and went away grieving, for he had many possessions.

Then Jesus looked around and said to his disciples, 'How hard it will be for those who have wealth to enter the kingdom of God!' And the disciples were perplexed at these words. But Jesus said to them again, 'Children, how hard it is to enter the kingdom of God! It is easier for a camel to go through the eye of a needle than for someone who is rich to enter the kingdom of God.' They were greatly astounded and said to one another, 'Then who can be saved?' Jesus looked at them and said, 'For mortals it is impossible, but not for God; for God all things are possible.'

Mark 10:17–27

'THE LAST WILL BE FIRST'

Peter began to say to him, 'Look, we have left everything and followed you.' Jesus said, 'Truly I tell you, there is no one who has left house or brothers or sisters or mother or father or children or fields, for my sake and for the sake of the good news, who will not receive a hundredfold now in this age — houses, brothers and sisters, mothers and children, and fields, with persecutions — and in the age to come eternal life. But many who are first will be last, and the last will be first.'

Mark 10:28–31

GREATNESS
AND SERVICE

James and John, the sons of Zebedee, came forward to him and said to him, 'Teacher, we want you to do for us whatever we ask of you.' And he said to them, 'What is it you want me to do for you?' And they said to him, 'Grant us to sit, one at your right hand and one at your left, in your glory.' But Jesus said to them, 'You do not know what you are asking. Are you able to drink the cup that I drink, or be baptized with the baptism that I am baptized with?' They replied, 'We are able.' Then Jesus said to them, 'The cup that I drink you will drink; and with the baptism with which I am baptized, you will be baptized; but to sit at my right hand or at my left is not mine to grant, but it is for those for whom it has been prepared.'

When the ten heard this, they began to be angry with James and John. So Jesus called them and said to them, 'You know that among the Gentiles those whom they recognize as their rulers lord it over them, and their great ones are tyrants over them. But it is not so among you; but whoever wishes to become great among you must be your servant, and whoever wishes to be first among you must be slave of all. For the Son of man came not to be served but to serve, and to give his life a ransom for many.'

Mark 10:35–45

'Have faith in God'

On the following day, when they came from Bethany, he was hungry. Seeing in the distance a fig tree in leaf, he went to see whether perhaps he would find anything on it. When he came to it, he found nothing but leaves, for it was not the season for figs. He said to it, 'May no one ever eat fruit from you again.' And his disciples heard it…

And when evening came, Jesus and his disciples went out of the city.

In the morning as they passed by, they saw the fig tree withered away to its roots.

Then Peter remembered and said to him, 'Rabbi, look! The fig tree that you cursed has withered.' Jesus answered them, 'Have faith in God. Truly I tell you, if you say to this mountain, "Be taken up and thrown into the sea", and if you do not doubt in your heart, but believe that what you say will come to pass, it will be done for you. So I tell you, whatever you ask for in prayer, believe that you have received it, and it will be yours.'

Mark 11:12–14, 19–24

'WHOEVER IS NOT AGAINST YOU'

John answered, 'Master, we saw someone casting out demons in your name, and we tried to stop him, because he does not follow with us.' But Jesus said to him, 'Do not stop him; for whoever is not against you is for you.'

Luke 9:49–50

'LET THE DEAD BURY THEIR OWN DEAD'

As they were going along the road, someone said to him, 'I will follow you wherever you go.' And Jesus said to him, 'Foxes have holes, and birds of the air have nests; but the Son of man has nowhere to lay his head.' To another he said, 'Follow me.' But he

said, 'Lord, first let me go and bury my father.' But Jesus said to him, 'Let the dead bury their own dead; but as for you, go and proclaim the kingdom of God.' Another said, 'I will follow you, Lord; but let me first say farewell to those at my home.' Jesus said to him, 'No one who puts a hand to the plough and looks back is fit for the kingdom of God.'

Luke 9:57–62

Satan's Fall

After this the Lord appointed seventy others and sent them on ahead of him in pairs to every town and place where he himself intended to go…

The seventy returned with joy, saying, 'Lord, in your name even the demons submit to us!' He said to them, 'I watched Satan fall from heaven like a flash of lightning. See, I have given you authority to tread on snakes and scorpions, and over all the power of the enemy; and nothing will hurt you. Nevertheless, do not rejoice at this, that the spirits submit to you, but rejoice that your names are written in heaven.'

Luke 10:1, 17–20

NO ONE KNOWS WHO THE MASTER IS

At that same hour Jesus rejoiced in the Holy Spirit and said, 'I thank you, Father, Lord of heaven and earth, because you have hidden these things from the wise and the intelligent and have revealed them to infants; yes, Father, for such was your gracious will. All things have been handed over to me by my Father; and no one knows who the Son is except the Father, or who the Father is except the Son and anyone to whom the Son chooses to reveal him.'

Then turning to the disciples, Jesus said to them privately, 'Blessed are the eyes that see what you see! For I tell you that many prophets and kings desired to see what you see, but did not see it, and to hear what you hear, but did not hear it.'

Luke 10:21–24

THE BETTER CHOICE

Now as they went on their way, he entered a certain village, where a woman named Martha welcomed him into her home. She had a sister named Mary, who sat at the Lord's feet and listened to what he was saying. But Martha was distracted by her many tasks; so she came to him and asked, 'Lord, do you not care that my sister has left me to do all the work by myself? Tell her then to help me.' But the Lord answered her, 'Martha, Martha, you are worried and distracted by many things; there is need of only one thing. Mary has chosen the better part, which will not be taken away from her.'

Luke 10:38–42

THE TEST OF DISCIPLESHIP

'For which of you, intending to build a tower, does not first sit down and estimate the cost, to see whether he has enough to complete it? Otherwise, when he has laid a foundation and is not able to finish, all who see it will begin to ridicule him, saying, "This fellow began to build and was not able to finish." Or what king, going out to wage war against another king, will not sit down first and consider whether he is able with ten thousand to oppose the one who comes against him with twenty thousand? If he cannot, then, while the other is still far away, he sends a delegation and asks for the terms of peace. So therefore, none of you can become my disciple if you do not give up all your possessions.'

Luke 14:28–33

'REMEMBER LOT'S WIFE'

Then he said to the disciples, 'The days are coming when you will long to see one of the days of the Son of man, and you will not see it. They will say to you, "Look there!" or "Look here!" Do not go, do not set off in pursuit. For as the lightning flashes and lights up the sky from one side to the other, so will the Son of man be in his day... Just as it was in the days of Lot: they were eating and drinking, buying and selling, planting and building, but on the day that Lot left Sodom, it rained fire and sulphur from heaven and destroyed all of them — it will be like that on the day that the Son of man is revealed. On that day, anyone on the housetop who has belongings in the house must not come down to take them away; and likewise anyone in the field must not turn back. Remember Lot's wife. Those who try to make their life secure will lose it, but those who lose their life will keep it. I tell you, on that night there will be two in one bed; one will be taken and the other left. There will be two women grinding meal together; one will be taken and the other left.' Then they asked him, 'Where, Lord?' He said to them, 'Where the corpse is, there the vultures will gather.'

Luke 17:22–24, 28–37

THE WIDOW'S MITE

He sat down opposite the treasury, and watched the crowd putting money into the treasury. Many rich people put in large sums. A poor widow came and put in two small copper coins, which are worth a penny. Then he called his disciples and said to them, 'Truly I tell you, this poor widow has put in more than all those who are contributing to the treasury. For all of them have contributed out of their abundance; but she out of her poverty has put in everything she had, all she had to live on.'

Mark 12:41–44

THE LITTLE APOCALYPSE

As he came out of the temple, one of his disciples said to him, 'Look, Teacher, what large stones and what large buildings!' Then Jesus asked him, 'Do you see these great buildings? Not one stone will be left here upon another; all will be thrown down.'

When he was sitting on the Mount of Olives opposite the temple, Peter, James, John, and Andrew asked him privately, 'Tell us, when will this be, and what will be the sign that all these things are about to be accomplished?' Then Jesus began to say to them, 'Beware that no one leads you astray. Many will come in my name and say, "I am he!" and they will lead many astray. When you hear of wars and rumours of wars, do not be alarmed; this must take place, but the end is still to come. For nation will rise against nation, and kingdom against kingdom; there will be earthquakes in various places; there will be famines. This is but the beginning of the birth pangs...

'But in those days, after that suffering,

the sun will be darkened,
and the moon will not give its light,
and the stars will be falling from heaven,
and the powers in the heavens will be shaken.

Then they will see "the Son of man coming in clouds" with great power and glory. Then he will send out the angels, and gather his elect from the four winds, from the ends of the earth to the ends of heaven.

'From the fig tree learn its lesson: as soon as its branch becomes tender and puts forth its leaves, you know that summer is near. So also, when you see these things taking place, you know that he is near, at the very gates. Truly I tell you, this generation will not pass away until all these things have taken place. Heaven and earth will pass away, but my words will not pass away.

'But about that day or hour no one knows, neither the angels in heaven, nor the Son, but only the Father. Beware, keep alert; for you do not know when the time will come. It is like a man going on a journey, when he leaves home and puts his slaves in charge, each with his work, and commands the doorkeeper to be on the watch. Therefore, keep awake — for you do not know when the master of the house will come, in the evening, or at midnight, or at cockcrow, or at dawn, or else he may find you asleep when he comes suddenly. And what I say to you I say to all: Keep awake.'

Mark 13:1–8, 24–37

Part Three

The Sermon on the Mount

When he saw the crowds he went up a
mountain. There he sat down, and when his
disciples had gathered round him he began
to address them. And this is the teaching
he gave...

Matthew 5:1–2

THE BEATITUDES

'Blessed are the poor in spirit;
the kingdom of Heaven is theirs.
Blessed are the sorrowful;
they shall find consolation.
Blessed are the gentle;
they shall have the earth for their possession.
Blessed are those who hunger and thirst
    to see right prevail;
they shall be satisfied.

Blessed are those
    who show mercy;
mercy shall be shown to them.
Blessed are those whose hearts are pure;
they shall see God.
Blessed are the peacemakers;
they shall be called God's children.
Blessed are those who are persecuted in
    the cause of right;
the kingdom of Heaven is theirs.

Blessed are you, when you suffer insults
and persecution and calumnies of every
kind for my sake. Exult and be glad, for
you have a rich reward in heaven; in the
same way they persecuted the prophets
before you.'

Matthew 5:3–12

SALT TO THE WORLD

'You are salt to the world. And if salt becomes tasteless, how is its saltness to be restored? It is good for nothing but to be thrown away and trodden underfoot.'

Matthew 5:13

LIGHT FOR ALL THE WORLD

'You are light for all the world. A town that stands on a hill cannot be hidden. When a lamp is lit, it is not put under the meal-tub, but on the lampstand, where it gives light to everyone in the house. Like the lamp, you must shed light among your fellows, so that, when they see the good you do, they may give praise to your Father in heaven.'

Matthew 5:14–16

THE COMPLETION OF THE LAW

'Do not suppose that I have come to abolish the law and the prophets; I did not come to abolish, but to complete. Truly I tell you: so long as heaven and earth endure, not a letter, not a dot, will disappear from the law until all that must happen has happened. Anyone therefore who sets aside even the least of the law's demands, and teaches others to do the same, will have the lowest place in the kingdom of Heaven, whereas anyone who keeps the law, and teaches others to do so, will rank high in the kingdom of Heaven. I tell you, unless you show yourselves far better than the scribes and Pharisees, you can never enter the kingdom of Heaven.'

Matthew 5:17–20

MURDER AND ANGER

'You have heard that our forefathers were told, "Do not commit murder; anyone who commits murder must be brought to justice." But what I tell you is this: Anyone who nurses anger against his brother must be brought to justice. Whoever calls his brother "good for nothing" deserves the sentence of the court; whoever calls him "fool" deserves hell-fire. So if you are presenting your gift at the altar and suddenly remember that your brother has a grievance against you, leave your gift where it is before the altar. First go and make your peace with your brother; then come back and offer your gift. If someone sues you, come to terms with him promptly while you are both on your way to court;

otherwise he may hand you over to the judge, and the judge to the officer, and you will be thrown into jail. Truly I tell you: once you are there you will not be let out until you have paid the last penny.'

Matthew 5:21–26

'You have heard that they were told, "Do not commit adultery." But what I tell you is this:

If a man looks at a woman with a lustful eye, he has already committed adultery with her in his heart. If your right eye causes your downfall, tear it out and fling it away; it is better for you to lose one part of your body than for the whole of it to be thrown into hell. If your right hand causes your downfall, cut it off and fling it away; it is better for you to lose one part of your body than for the whole of it to go to hell.'

Matthew 5:27–30

DIVORCE

'They were told, "A man who
divorces his wife must give her
a certificate of dismissal."
But what I tell you is
this: If a man divorces
his wife for any cause
other than unchastity
he involves her in
adultery; and whoever
marries her commits
adultery.'

Matthew 5:31–32

SWEARING OATHS

'Again, you have heard that our
forefathers were told, "Do
not break your oath," and
"Oaths sworn to the
Lord must be kept."
But what I tell you is
this: You are not to
swear at all – not by
heaven, for it is God's
throne, nor by the
earth, for it is his
footstool, nor by
Jerusalem, for it is the city of
the great King, nor by your own
head, because you cannot turn one hair of it
white or black. Plain "Yes" or "No" is all
you need to say; anything beyond that comes
from the evil one.'

Matthew 5:33–37

THE EXTRA MILE

'You have heard that they were told, "An eye for an eye, a tooth for a tooth." But what I tell you is this: Do not resist those who wrong you. If anyone slaps you on the right cheek, turn and offer him the other also. If anyone wants to sue you and takes your shirt, let him have your cloak as well. If someone in authority presses you into service for one mile, go with him two. Give to anyone who asks; and do not turn your back on anyone who wants to borrow.'

Matthew 5:38–42

'LOVE YOUR ENEMIES'

'You have heard that they were told, "Love your neighbour and hate your enemy." But what I tell you is this: Love your enemies and pray for your persecutors; only so can you be children of your heavenly Father, who causes the sun to rise on good and bad alike, and sends the rain on the innocent and the wicked. If you love only those who love you, what reward can you expect? Even the tax-collectors do as much as that. If you greet only your brothers, what is there extraordinary about that? Even the heathen do as much. There must be no limit to your goodness, as your heavenly Father's goodness knows no bounds.'

Matthew 5:43–48

ALMSGIVING

'Be careful not to parade your religion before others; if you do, no reward awaits you with your Father in heaven.

    'So, when you give alms, do not announce it with a flourish of trumpets, as the hypocrites do in synagogues and in the streets to win the praise of others. Truly I tell you; they have their reward already. But when you give alms, do not let your left hand know what your right is doing; your good deed must be secret, and your Father who sees what is done in secret will reward you.'

Matthew 6:1–4

Prayer

'Again, when you pray, do not be like the hypocrites; they love to say their prayers standing up in synagogues and at street corners for everyone to see them. Truly I tell you: they have their reward already. But when you pray, go into a room by yourself, shut the door, and pray to your Father who is in secret; and your Father who sees what is done in secret will reward you.

'In your prayers do not go babbling on like the heathen, who imagine that the more they say the more likely they are to be heard. Do not imitate them, for your Father knows what your needs are before you ask him.'

Matthew 6:5–8

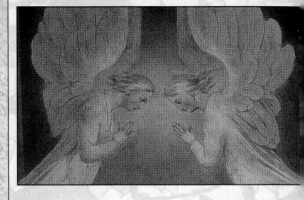

The Master's prayer

'This is how you should pray:

Our Father in heaven,
may your name be hallowed;
your kingdom come,
your will be done,
on earth as in heaven.
Give us today our daily bread.
Forgive us the wrong we have done,
as we have forgiven those who have wronged us.
And do not put us to the test,
but save us from the evil one.'

Matthew 6:9–13

FORGIVENESS

'For if you forgive others the wrongs they have done, your heavenly Father will also forgive you; but if you do not forgive others, then your Father will not forgive the wrongs that you have done.'

Matthew 6:14–15

FASTING

'So too when you fast, do not look gloomy like the hypocrites: they make their faces unsightly so that everybody may see that they are fasting. Truly I tell you: they have their reward already. But when you fast, anoint your head and wash your face, so that no one sees that you are fasting, but only your Father who is in secret; and your Father who sees what is done in secret will give you your reward.'

Matthew 6:16–18

TREASURE ON EARTH

'Do not store up for
yourselves treasure on
earth, where moth and
rust destroy, and thieves
break in and steal; but
store up treasure in
heaven, where neither
moth nor rust will
destroy, nor thieves
break in and steal. For
where your treasure is,
there will your heart be
also.'

Matthew 6:19–21

'No one can serve two masters'

'No one can serve two masters; for either he will hate the first and love the second, or he will be devoted to the first and despise the second. You cannot serve God and Money.'

Matthew 6:24

The lamp of the body

'The lamp of the body is the eye. If your eyes are sound, you will have light for your whole body; if your eyes are bad, your whole body will be in darkness. If then the only light you have is darkness, how great a darkness that will be.'

Matthew 6:22–23

'DO NOT BE ANXIOUS'

'This is why I tell you not to be anxious
about food and drink to keep you alive and
about clothes to cover your body. Surely life
is more than food, the body more than
clothes. Look at the birds in the sky; they
do not sow and reap
and store in barns, yet
your heavenly Father
feeds them. Are you
not worth more than
the birds? Can anxious
thought add a single
day to your life? And
why be anxious about
clothes? Consider how
the lilies grow in the
fields; they do not
work, they do not
spin; yet I tell you, even Solomon in all his
splendour was not attired like one of them.
If that is how God clothes the grass in the

fields, which is there today and tomorrow is thrown on the stove, will he not all the more clothe you? How little faith you have! Do not ask anxiously, "What are we to eat? What are we to drink? What shall we wear?" These are the things that occupy the minds of the heathen, but your heavenly Father knows that you need them all. Set your mind on God's kingdom and his justice before everything else, and all the rest will come to you as well. So do not be anxious about tomorrow; tomorrow will look after itself. Each day has troubles enough of its own.'

Matthew 6:25–34

'Do not judge'

'Do not judge, and you will not be judged. For as you judge others, so you will yourselves be judged, and whatever measure you deal out to others will be dealt to you. Why do you look at the speck of sawdust in your brother's eye, with never a thought for the plank in your own? How can you say to your brother, "Let me take the speck out of your eye," when all the time there is a plank in your own? You hypocrite! First take the plank out of your own eye, and then you will see clearly to take the speck out of your brother's.'

Matthew 7:1–5

PEARLS TO THE PIGS

'Do not give dogs what is holy; do not
throw your pearls to the pigs: they will
only trample on them, and turn and tear
you to pieces.'

Matthew 7:6

'SEEK, AND YOU WILL FIND'

'Ask, and you will receive; seek, and you will find; knock, and the door will be opened to you. For everyone who asks receives, those who seek find, and to those who knock, the door will be opened.

'Would any of you offer his son a stone when he asks for bread, or a snake when he asks for a fish? If you, bad as you are, know how to give good things to your children, how much more will your heavenly Father give good things to those who ask him!'

Matthew 7:7–11

THE GOLDEN RULE

'Always treat others as you would like them to treat you: that is the law and the prophets.'

Matthew 7:12

'Enter by the narrow gate'

'Enter by the narrow gate. Wide is the gate and broad the road that leads to destruction, and many enter that way; narrow is the gate and constricted the road that leads to life, and those who find them are few.'

Matthew 7:13–14

Wolves in sheep's clothing

'Beware of false prophets, who come to you dressed up as sheep while underneath they are savage wolves.'

Matthew 7:15

GOOD AND BAD FRUIT

'You will recognize them by
their fruit. Can grapes be
picked from briars, or figs
from thistles? A good tree
always yields sound fruit, and
a poor tree bad fruit. A good
tree cannot bear bad fruit, or a poor
tree sound fruit. A tree that does not yield
sound fruit is cut down and thrown on the
fire. That is why I say you will recognize
them by their fruit.'

Matthew 7:16–20

'I NEVER KNEW YOU'

'Not everyone who says to me, "Lord, Lord" will enter the kingdom of Heaven, but only those who do the will of my heavenly Father. When the day comes, many will say to me,

WISE AND FOOLISH BUILDERS

'So whoever hears these words of mine and acts on them is like a man who had the sense to build his house on rock. The rain came down, the floods rose, the winds blew and beat upon that house; but it did not fall, because its foundations were on rock. And whoever hears these words of mine and does not act on them is like a man who was foolish enough to build his house on sand. The rain came down, the floods rose, the winds blew and battered against that house; and it fell with a great crash.'

Matthew 7:24–27

"Lord, Lord, did we not prophesy in your name, drive out demons in your name, and in your name perform many miracles?" Then I will tell them plainly, "I never knew you. Out of my sight; your deeds are evil!"'

Matthew 7:21–23

When Jesus had finished this discourse the people were amazed at his teaching; unlike their scribes he taught with a note of authority.

Matthew 7:28–29

Proverbs and Shorter Sayings

A LAMP UNDER A BOWL

He said to them, 'Do you bring in a lamp to put it under a bowl or a bed? Instead, don't you put it on its stand? For whatever is hidden is meant to be disclosed, and whatever is concealed is meant to be brought out into the open.'

Mark 4:21–22

'REPENT AND BELIEVE'

'The time has come,' he said. 'The kingdom of God is near. Repent and believe the good news!'

Mark 1:15

The seed of the kingdom

He also said, 'This is what the kingdom of God is like. A man scatters seed on the ground. Night and day, whether he sleeps or gets up, the seed sprouts and grows, though he does not know how. All by itself the soil produces corn — first the stalk, then the ear, then the full grain in the ear. As soon as the grain is ripe, he puts the sickle to it, because the harvest has come.'

Mark 4:26–29

A mustard seed

Again he said, 'What shall we say the kingdom of God is like, or what parable shall we use to describe it? It is like a mustard seed, which is the smallest seed you plant in the ground. Yet when planted, it grows and becomes the largest of all garden plants, with such big branches that the birds of the air can perch in its shade.'

Mark 4:30–32

A PROPHET WITHOUT HONOUR

Jesus said to them, 'Only in his home town, among his relatives and in his own house is a prophet without honour.'

Mark 6:4

SALT OF THE GOSPEL

'Salt is good, but if it loses its saltiness, how can you make it salty again? Have salt in yourselves, and be at peace with each other.'

Mark 9:50

PRAYER AND FORGIVENESS

'And when you stand praying, if you hold anything against anyone, forgive him, so that your Father in heaven may forgive you your sins. [But if you do not forgive, neither will your Father who is in heaven forgive your sins.]'

Mark 11:25–26

'MY BURDEN IS LIGHT'

'Come to me, all you who are weary and burdened, and I will give you rest. Take my yoke upon you and learn from me, for I am gentle and humble in heart, and you will find rest for your souls. For my yoke is easy and my burden is light.'

Matthew 11:28–30

Yeast

He told them still another parable: 'The kingdom of heaven is like yeast that a woman took and mixed into a large amount of flour until it worked all through the dough.'

Matthew 13:33

Hidden treasure

'The kingdom of heaven is like treasure hidden in a field. When a man found it, he hid it again, and then in his joy went and sold all he had and bought that field.'

Matthew 13:44

The pearl of great value

'Again, the kingdom of heaven is like a merchant looking for fine pearls. When he found one of great value, he went away and sold everything he had and bought it.'

Matthew 13:45–46

The Dragnet

'Once again, the kingdom of heaven is like a net that was let down into the lake and caught all kinds of fish.
When it was full, the fishermen pulled it up on the shore. Then they sat down and collected the good fish in baskets, but threw the bad away.
This is how it will be at the end of the age.

The angels will come and separate the wicked from the righteous and throw them into the fiery furnace, where there will be weeping and gnashing of teeth.'

Matthew 13:47–50

New and Old Treasure

He said to them, 'Therefore every teacher of the law who has been instructed about the kingdom of heaven is like the owner of a house who brings out of his storeroom new treasures as well as old.'

Matthew 13:52

FOUR WOES

'But woe to you who are rich,
*   for you have already received your comfort.*
Woe to you who are well fed now,
*   for you will go hungry.*
Woe to you who laugh now,
*   for you will mourn and weep.*
Woe to you when all men
*   speak well of you,*
*   for that is how their fathers*
treated the false prophets.'

Luke 6:24–26

MEASURE FOR MEASURE

'Do not judge, and you will not be judged.
Do not condemn, and you will not be
condemned. Forgive, and you will be
forgiven. Give, and it will be given to you.
    A good measure, pressed down, shaken
            together and running over, will
                be poured into your lap.
                For with the measure
                you use, it will be
                measured to you.'

Luke 6:37–38

THE BLIND LEADING THE BLIND

He also told them this parable: 'Can a blind man lead a blind man? Will they not both fall into a pit?'

Luke 6:39

A STUDENT AND HIS TEACHER

'A student is not above his teacher, but everyone who is fully trained will be like his teacher.'

Luke 6:40

TRUE FAMILY

Now Jesus' mother and brothers came to see him, but they were not able to get near him because of the crowd. Someone told him, 'Your mother and brothers are standing outside, wanting to see you.'

He replied, 'My mother and brothers are those who hear God's word and put it into practice.'

Luke 8:19–21

TRUE BLESSING

As Jesus was saying these things, a woman in the crowd called out, 'Blessed is the mother who gave you birth and nursed you.'

He replied, 'Blessed rather are those who hear the word of God and obey it.'

Luke 11:27–28

GUARD AGAINST ALL GREED

Someone in the crowd said to him, 'Teacher, tell my brother to divide the inheritance with me.'

Jesus replied, 'Man, who appointed me a judge or an arbiter between you?' Then he said to them, 'Watch out! Be on your guard against all kinds of greed; a man's life does not consist in the abundance of his possessions.'

Luke 12:13–15

'Unless you repent'

Now there were some present at that time who told Jesus about the Galileans whose blood Pilate had mixed with their sacrifices. Jesus answered, 'Do you think that these Galileans were worse sinners than all the other Galileans because they suffered this way? I tell you, no! But unless you repent, you too will all perish. Or those eighteen who died when the tower in Siloam fell on them – do you think they were more guilty than all the others living in Jerusalem? I tell you, no! But unless you repent, you too will all perish.'

Luke 13:1–5

True honour

'When someone invites you to a wedding feast, do not take the place of honour, for a person more distinguished than you may have been invited. If so, the host who invited both of you will come and say to you, "Give this man your seat." Then, humiliated, you will have to take the least important place. But when you are invited, take the lowest place, so that when your host comes, he will say to you, "Friend, move up to a better place." Then you will be honoured in the presence of all your fellow guests. For everyone who exalts himself will be humbled, and he who humbles himself will be exalted.'

Luke 14:8–11

TRUE GENEROSITY

Then Jesus said to his host, 'When you give a luncheon or dinner, do not invite your friends, your brothers or relatives, or your rich neighbours; if you do, they may invite you back and so you will be repaid. But when you give a banquet, invite the poor, the crippled, the lame, the blind, and you will be blessed. Although they cannot repay you, you will be repaid at the resurrection of the righteous.'

Luke 14:12–14

TRUE TRUSTWORTHINESS

'Whoever can be trusted with very little can also be trusted with much, and whoever is dishonest with very little will also be dishonest with much. So if you have not been trustworthy in handling worldly wealth, who will trust you with true riches? And if you have not been trustworthy with someone else's property, who will give you property of your own?'

Luke 16:10–12

A SERVANT'S DUTY

'Suppose one of you had a servant ploughing or looking after the sheep. Would he say to the servant when he comes in from the field, "Come along now and sit down to eat"? Would he not rather say, "Prepare my supper, get yourself ready and wait on me while I eat and drink; after that you may eat and drink"? Would he thank the servant because he did what he was told to do? So you also, when you have done everything you were told to do, should say, "We are unworthy servants; we have only done our duty."'

Luke 17:7–10

THE KINGDOM WITHIN

Once, having been asked by the Pharisees when the kingdom of God would come, Jesus replied, 'The kingdom of God does not come with your careful observation, nor will people say, "Here it is," or "There it is," because the kingdom of God is within you.'

Luke 17:20–21

Part Five

The Major Parables

THE SOWER

On another occasion he began to teach by the lakeside. The crowd that gathered round him was so large that he had to get into a boat on the lake and sit there, with the whole crowd on the beach right down to the water's edge. And he taught them many things by parables.

As he taught he said:

'Listen! A sower went out to sow. And it happened that as he sowed, some of the seed fell along the footpath; and the birds came and ate it up. Some fell on rocky ground, where it had little soil, and it sprouted quickly because it had no depth of earth; but when the sun rose it was scorched, and as it had no root it withered away. Some fell among thistles; and the thistles grew up and choked the corn, and it produced no crop. And some of the seed fell into good soil, where it came up and grew, and produced a crop; and the yield was thirtyfold, sixtyfold, even a hundredfold.' He added, 'If you have ears to hear, then hear.'

When Jesus was alone with the Twelve and his other companions they questioned him about the parables. He answered, 'To you the secret of the kingdom of God has been given; but to those who are outside, everything comes by way of parables, so that (as scripture says) they may look and look, but see nothing; they may listen and listen, but understand nothing; otherwise they might turn to God and be forgiven.'

He went on: 'Do you not understand has been sown in them. With others the seed falls on rocky ground; as soon as they hear the word, they accept it with joy, but it strikes no root in them; they have no

this parable? How then are you to understand any parable? The sower sows the word. With some the seed falls along the footpath; no sooner have they heard it than Satan comes and carries off the word which staying-power, and when there is trouble or persecution on account of the word, they quickly lose faith. With others again the seed falls among thistles; they hear the word, but worldly cares and the false glamour of wealth and evil desires of all kinds come in and choke the word, and it proves barren. But there are some with whom the seed is sown on good soil; they accept the word when they hear it, and they bear fruit thirtyfold, sixtyfold, or a hundredfold.'

Mark 4:1–20

The Wheat and the Darnel

Here is another parable he gave them: 'The kingdom of Heaven is like this. A man sowed his field with good seed; but while everyone was asleep his enemy came, sowed darnel among the wheat, and made off. When the corn sprouted and began to fill out, the darnel could be seen among it. The farmer's men went to their master and said, "Sir, was it not good seed that you sowed in your field? So where has the darnel come from?" "This is an enemy's doing," he replied. "Well then," they said, "shall we go and gather the darnel?" "No," he answered; "in gathering it you might pull up the wheat at the same time. Let them both grow together till harvest; and at harvest time I will tell the reapers, 'Gather the darnel first, and tie it in bundles for burning; then collect the wheat into my barn.'"...

Then he sent the people away, and went into the house, where his disciples came to him and said, 'Explain to us the parable of the darnel in the field.' He replied, 'The sower of the good seed is the Son of man. The field is the world; the good seed stands for the children of the Kingdom, the darnel for the children of the evil one, and the enemy who sowed the darnel is the devil. The harvest is the end of time, and the reapers are angels. As the darnel is gathered up and burnt, so at the end of time the Son of man will send his angels, who will gather out of his kingdom every cause of sin, and all whose deeds are evil; these will be thrown into the blazing furnace, where there will be wailing and grinding of teeth. Then the righteous will shine like the sun in the kingdom of their Father. If you have ears, then hear.'

Matthew 13:24–30, 36–43

The unforgiving servant

'The kingdom of Heaven, therefore, should be thought of in this way: There was once a king who decided to settle accounts with the men who served him. At the outset there appeared before him a man who owed ten thousand talents. Since he had no means of paying, his master ordered him to be sold, with his wife, his children, and everything he had, to meet the debt. The man fell at his master's feet. "Be patient with me," he implored, "and I will pay you in full"; and the master was so moved with pity that he let the man go and cancelled the debt. But no sooner had the man gone out than he met a fellow-servant who owed him a hundred denarii; he took hold of him, seizing him by the throat, and said, "Pay me what you owe." The man fell at his fellow-servant's feet, and begged him, "Be patient with me, and I will pay you"; but he refused, and had him thrown into jail until he should pay the debt. The other servants were deeply distressed when they saw what had happened, and they went to their master and told him the whole story. Then he sent for the man and said,

"You scoundrel! I cancelled the whole of your debt when you appealed to me; ought you not to have shown mercy to your fellow-servant just as I showed mercy to you?" And so angry was the master that he condemned the man to be tortured until he should pay the debt in full. That is how my heavenly Father will deal with you, unless you each forgive your brother from your hearts.'

Matthew 18:23–35

THE LABOURERS IN THE VINEYARD

'The kingdom of Heaven is like this. There was once a landowner who went out early one morning to hire labourers for his vineyard; and after agreeing to pay them the usual day's wage he sent them off to work. Three hours later he went out again and saw some more men standing idle in the market-place. "Go and join the others in the vineyard," he said, "and I will pay you a fair wage"; so off they went. At midday he went out again, and at three in the afternoon, and made the same arrangement as before. An hour before sunset he went out and found another group standing there; so he said to them, "Why are you standing here all day doing nothing?" "Because no one has hired us," they replied; so he told them, "Go and join the others in the vineyard." When evening fell, the owner of the vineyard said to the overseer, "Call the labourers and give them their pay, beginning with those who came last and ending with the first." Those who had started work an hour before sunset came forward, and were paid the full day's wage. When it was the turn of the men who had come first, they expected something extra, but were paid the same as the others. As they took it, they grumbled at their employer: "These latecomers did only one hour's work, yet you have treated them on a level with us, who have sweated the whole day long in the blazing sun!" The owner turned to one of them and said, "My friend, I am not being unfair to you. You agreed on the usual wage for the day, did you not? Take your pay and go home. I choose to give the last man the same as you. Surely I am free to do what I like with my own money? Why be jealous because I am generous?" So the last will be first, and the first last.'

Matthew 20:1–16

The wicked tenants

'Listen to another parable. There was a landowner who planted a vineyard: he put a wall round it, hewed out a winepress, and built a watch-tower; then he let it out to vine-growers and went abroad. When the harvest season approached, he sent his servants to the tenants to collect the produce due to him. But they seized his servants, thrashed one, killed another, and stoned a third. Again, he sent other servants, this time a larger number; and they treated them in the same way. Finally he sent his son. "They will respect my son," he said. But when they saw the son the tenants said to one another, "This is the heir; come on, let us kill him, and get his inheritance." So they seized him, flung him out of the vineyard, and killed him. When the owner of the vineyard comes, how do you think he will deal with those tenants?' 'He will bring those bad men to a bad end,' they answered, 'and hand the vineyard over to other tenants, who will give him his share of the crop when the season comes.' Jesus said to them, 'Have you never read in the scriptures: "The stone which the builders rejected has become the main corner-stone. This is the Lord's doing, and it is wonderful in our eyes"? Therefore, I tell you, the kingdom of God will be taken away from you, and given to a nation that yields the proper fruit.'

When the chief priests and Pharisees heard his parables, they saw that he was referring to them. They wanted to arrest him, but were afraid of the crowds, who looked on Jesus as a prophet.

Matthew 21:33–46

THE WISE AND FOOLISH BRIDESMAIDS

'When the day comes, the kingdom of Heaven will be like this. There were ten girls, who took their lamps and went out to meet the bridegroom. Five of them were foolish, and five prudent; when the foolish ones took their lamps, they took no oil with them, but the others took flasks of oil with their lamps. As the bridegroom was a long time in coming, they all dozed off to sleep. But at midnight there came a shout: "Here is the bridegroom! Come out to meet him." Then the girls all got up and trimmed their lamps. The foolish said to the prudent, "Our lamps are going out; give us some of your oil." "No," they answered; "there will never be enough for all of us. You had better go to the dealers and buy some for yourselves." While they were away the bridegroom arrived; those who were ready went in with him to the wedding banquet; and the door was shut. Later the others came back. "Sir, sir, open the door for us," they cried. But he answered, "Truly I tell you: I do not know you." Keep awake then, for you know neither the day nor the hour.'

Matthew 25:1–13

THE USELESS SERVANT

'[The kingdom of heaven] is like a man going abroad, who called his servants and entrusted his capital to them; to one he gave five bags of gold, to another two, to another one, each according to his ability. Then he left the country. The man who had the five bags went at once and employed them in business, and made a profit of five bags, and the man who had the two bags made two. But the man who had been given one bag of gold went off and dug a hole in the ground, and hid his master's money. A long time afterwards their master returned, and proceeded to settle accounts with them. The man who had been given the five bags of gold came and produced the five he had made: "Master," he said, "you left five bags with me; look, I have made five more." "Well done, good and faithful servant!" said the master. "You have proved trustworthy in a small matter; I will now put you in charge of something big. Come and share your master's joy." The man with the two bags then came and said, "Master, you left two

bags with me; look, I have made two more."
"Well done, good and faithful servant!" said
the master. "You have proved trustworthy in
a small matter; I will now put you in charge
of something big. Come and share your
master's joy." Then the man who had been
given one bag came and said, "Master, I
knew you to be a hard man: you reap where
you have not sown, you gather where you
have not scattered; so I was afraid, and I
went and hid your gold in the ground. Here
it is — you have what belongs to you." "You
worthless, lazy servant!" said the master.
"You knew, did you, that I reap where I
have not sown, and gather where I have
not scattered? Then you ought to have put
my money on deposit, and on my return I
should have got it back with interest. Take
the bag of gold from him, and give it to the
one with the ten bags. For everyone who has
will be given more, till he has enough and
to spare; and everyone who has nothing will
forfeit even what he has. As for the useless
servant, throw him out into the dark, where
there will be wailing and grinding of teeth!"'

Matthew 25:14–30

THE SHEEP AND THE GOATS

'When the Son of man comes in his glory
and all the angels with him, he will sit on
his glorious throne, with all the nations
gathered before him. He will separate people
into two groups, as a shepherd separates the
sheep from the goats; he will place the sheep
on his right hand and the goats on his left.
Then the king will say to those on his right,
"You have my Father's blessing; come, take
possession of the kingdom that has been
ready for you since the world was made. For
when I was hungry, you gave me food; when
thirsty, you gave me drink; when I was a
stranger, you took me into your home; when
naked, you clothed me; when I was ill, you
came to my help; when in prison, you visited

me." Then the righteous will reply, "Lord, when was it that we saw you hungry and fed you, or thirsty and gave you drink, a stranger and took you home, or naked and clothed you? When did we see you ill or in prison, and come to visit you?" And the king will answer, "Truly I tell you: anything you did for one of my brothers here, however insignificant, you did for me." Then he will say to those on his left, "A curse is on you; go from my sight to the

eternal fire that is ready for the devil and his angels. For when I was hungry, you gave me nothing to eat; when thirsty, nothing to drink; when I was a stranger, you did not welcome me; when I was naked, you did not clothe me; when I was ill and in prison, you did not come to my help." And they in their turn will reply, "Lord, when was it that we saw you hungry or thirsty or a stranger or naked or ill or in prison, and did nothing for you?" And he will answer, "Truly I tell you: anything you failed to do for one of these, however insignificant, you failed to do for me." And they will go away to eternal punishment, but the righteous will enter eternal life.'

Matthew
25:31–46

The good Samaritan

A lawyer once came forward to test him by asking: 'Teacher, what must I do to inherit eternal life?' Jesus said, 'What is written in the law? What is your reading of it?' He replied, 'Love the Lord your God with all your heart, and with all your soul, with all your strength, and with all your mind; and your neighbour as yourself.' 'That is the right answer,' said Jesus; 'do that and you will have life.'

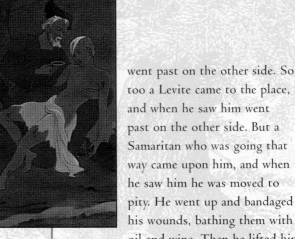

Wanting to justify his question, he asked, 'But who is my neighbour?' Jesus replied, 'A man was on his way from Jerusalem down to Jericho when he was set upon by robbers, who stripped and beat him, and went off leaving him half dead. It so happened that a priest was going down by the same road, and when he saw him, he went past on the other side. So too a Levite came to the place, and when he saw him went past on the other side. But a Samaritan who was going that way came upon him, and when he saw him he was moved to pity. He went up and bandaged his wounds, bathing them with oil and wine. Then he lifted him on to his own beast, brought him to an inn, and looked after him. Next day he produced two silver pieces and gave them to the innkeeper, and said, "Look after him; and if you spend more, I will repay you on my way back." Which of these three do you think was neighbour to the man who fell into the hands of the robbers?' He answered, 'The one who showed him kindness.' Jesus said to him, 'Go and do as he did.'

Luke 10:25–37

THE RICH FOOL

And he told them this parable: 'There was a rich man whose land yielded a good harvest. He debated with himself: "What am I to do? I have not the space to store my produce. This is what I will do," said he: "I will pull down my barns and build them bigger. I will collect in them all my grain and other goods, and I will say to myself, 'You have plenty of good things laid by, enough for many years to come: take life easy, eat, drink, and enjoy yourself.'" But God said to him, "You fool, this very night you must surrender your life; and the money you have made, who will get it now?" That is how it is with the man who piles up treasure for himself and remains a pauper in the sight of God.'

Luke 12:16–21

The trusty steward

The Lord said, 'Who is the trusty and
sensible man whom his master will appoint
as his steward, to manage
his servants and issue
their rations at the proper
time? Happy that servant
if his master comes home
and finds him at work!
I tell you this: he will be
put in charge of all his
master's property. But
if that servant says to
himself, "The master is
a long time coming,"
and begins to bully the
menservants and maids,
and to eat and drink and
get drunk, then the
master will arrive on a day
when the servant does not expect him, at a
time he has not been told. He will cut him
in pieces and assign him a
place among the faithless.

'The servant who
knew his master's wishes,
yet made no attempt to
carry them out, will be
flogged severely. But one
who did not know them
and earned a beating will
be flogged less severely.
Where someone has been
given much, much will be
expected of him; and the
more he has had entrusted
to him the more will be
demanded of him.'

Luke 12:42–48

THE BIG DINNER PARTY

Hearing this one of the company said to him, 'Happy are those who will sit at the feast in the kingdom of God!' Jesus answered, 'A man was giving a big dinner party and had sent out many invitations. At dinner-time he sent his servant to tell his guests, "Come please, everything is now ready." One after another they all sent excuses. The first said, "I have bought a piece of land, and I must go and inspect it; please accept my apologies." The second said, "I have bought five yoke of oxen, and I am on my way to try them out; please accept my apologies." The next said, "I cannot come; I have just got married." When the servant came back he reported this to his master. The master of the house was furious and said to him, "Go out quickly into the streets and alleys of the town, and bring in the poor, the crippled, the blind, and the lame." When the servant informed him that his orders had been carried out and there was still room, his master replied, "Go out on the highways and along the hedgerows and compel them to come in; I want my house full. I tell you, not one of those who were invited shall taste my banquet."'

Luke 14:15–24

THE WEDDING BANQUET

Jesus spoke to them again in parables: 'The kingdom of Heaven is like this. There was a king who arranged a banquet for his son's wedding; but when he sent his servants to summon the guests he had invited, they refused to come. Then he sent other servants, telling them to say to the guests, "Look! I have prepared this banquet for you. My bullocks and fatted beasts have been slaughtered, and everything is ready. Come to the wedding." But they took no notice; one went off to his farm, another to his business, and the others seized the servants, attacked them brutally, and killed them. The king was furious; he sent troops to put those murderers to death and set their town on fire. Then he said to his servants, "The wedding banquet is ready; but the guests I invited did not deserve the honour. Go out therefore to the main thoroughfares, and invite everyone you can find to the wedding." The servants went out into the streets, and collected everyone they could find, good and bad alike. So the hall was packed with guests.

'When the king came in to watch them feasting, he observed a man who was not dressed for a wedding. "My friend," said the king, "how do you come to be here without wedding clothes?" But he had nothing to say. The king then said to his attendants, "Bind him hand and foot; fling him out into the dark, the place of wailing and grinding of teeth." For many are invited, but few are chosen.'

Matthew 22:1–14

THE LOST SHEEP

'If one of you has a hundred sheep and loses one of them, does he not leave the ninety-nine in the wilderness and go after the one that is missing until he finds it? And when he does, he lifts it joyfully on to his shoulders, and goes home to call his friends and neighbours together. "Rejoice with me!" he cries. "I have found my lost sheep." In the same way, I tell you, there will be greater joy in heaven over one sinner who repents than over ninety-nine righteous people who do not need to repent.'

Luke 15:4–7

THE LOST COIN

'Or again, if a woman has ten silver coins and loses one of them, does she not light the lamp, sweep out the house, and look in every corner till she finds it? And when she does, she calls her friends and neighbours together, and says, "Rejoice with me! I have found the coin that I lost." In the same way, I tell you, there is joy among the angels of God over one sinner who repents.'

Luke 15:8–10

THE PRODIGAL SON

Again he said: 'There was once a man who had two sons; and the younger said to his father, "Father, give me my share of the property." So he divided his estate between them. A few days later the younger son turned the whole of his share into cash and left home for a distant country, where he squandered it in dissolute living. He had spent it all, when a severe famine fell upon that country and he began to be in need. So he went and attached himself to one of the local landowners, who sent him on to his farm to mind the pigs. He would have been glad to fill his belly with the pods that the pigs were eating, but no one gave him anything.

'Then he came to his senses: "How many of my father's hired servants have more food than they can eat," he said, "and here am I, starving to death! I will go at once to my father, and say to him, 'Father, I have sinned against God and against you; I am no longer fit to be called your son; treat me as one of your hired servants.'" So he set out for his father's house. But while he was still a long way off his father saw him, and his heart went out to him; he ran to meet him, flung his arms round him, and kissed him. The son said, "Father, I have sinned against God and finger and sandals on his feet. Bring the fatted calf and kill it, and let us celebrate with a feast. For this son of mine was dead

against you; I am no longer fit to be called your son." But the father said to his servants, "Quick! Fetch a robe, the best we have, and put it on him; put a ring on his and has come back to life; he was lost and is found." And the festivities began.

'Now the elder son had been out on the farm; and on his way back, as he approached the house, he heard music and dancing. He called one of the servants and asked what it meant. The servant told him, "Your brother has come home, and your father has killed the fatted calf because he has him back safe and sound." But he was angry and refused to go in. His father came out and pleaded with him; but he retorted, "You know how I have slaved for you all these years; I never once disobeyed your orders; yet you never gave me so much as a kid, to celebrate with my friends. But now that this son of yours turns up, after running through your money with his women, you kill the fatted calf for him."

"My boy," said the father, "you are always with me, and everything I have is yours. How could we fail to celebrate this happy day? Your brother here was dead and has come back to life; he was lost and has been found.'"

Luke 15:11–32

THE DISHONEST STEWARD

He said to his disciples, 'There was a rich man who had a steward, and he received complaints that this man was squandering the property. So he sent for him, and said, "What is this that I hear about you? Produce your accounts, for you cannot be steward any longer." The steward said to himself, "What am I to do now that my master is going to dismiss me from my post? I am not strong enough to dig, and I am too proud to beg. I know what I must do, to make sure that, when I am dismissed, there will be people who will take me into their homes." He summoned his master's debtors one by one. To the first he said, "How much do you owe my master?" He replied, "A hundred jars of olive oil." He said, "Here is your account. Sit down and make it fifty, and be quick about it." Then he said to another, "And you, how much do you owe?" He said, "A hundred measures of wheat," and was told, "Here is your account; make it eighty." And the master applauded the dishonest steward for acting so astutely. For in dealing with their own kind the children of this world are more astute than the children of light.

'So I say to you, use your worldly wealth to win friends for yourselves, so that when money is a thing of the past you may be received into an eternal home.'

Luke 16:1–9

The rich man and Lazarus

'There was once a rich man, who used to dress in purple and the finest linen, and feasted sumptuously every day. At his gate lay a poor man named Lazarus, who was covered with sores. He would have been glad

to satisfy his hunger with the scraps from the rich man's table. Dogs used to come and lick his sores. One day the poor man died and was carried away by the angels to be with Abraham. The rich man also died and was buried. In Hades, where he was in torment, he looked up and there, far away, was Abraham with Lazarus close beside him. "Abraham, my father," he called out, "take pity on me! Send Lazarus to dip the tip of his finger in water, to cool my tongue, for I am in agony in this fire." But Abraham said, "My child, remember that the good things fell to you in your lifetime, and the bad to Lazarus. Now he has his consolation here and it is you who are in agony. But that is not all: there is a great gulf fixed between us; no one can cross it from our side to reach you, and none may pass from your side to us." "Then, father," he replied, "will you send him to my father's house, where I have five brothers, to warn them, so that they may not come to this place of torment?" But Abraham said, "They have Moses and the prophets; let them listen to them." "No, father Abraham," he replied, "but if someone from the dead visits them, they will repent." Abraham answered, "If they do not listen to Moses and the prophets they will pay no heed even if someone should rise from the dead."'

Luke 16:19–31

THE IMPORTUNATE WIDOW ·

He told them a parable to show that they
should keep on praying and never lose heart:
'In a certain city there was a judge who had
no fear of God or respect for man, and in
the same city there was a widow who kept
coming before him to demand justice against
her opponent. For a time he refused; but in
the end he said to himself, "Although I have
no fear of God or respect for man, yet this
widow is so great a nuisance that I will give
her justice before she wears me out with her
persistence."' The Lord said, 'You hear what
the unjust judge says. Then will not God
give justice to his chosen, to whom he
listens patiently while they cry out to him
day and night? I tell you, he will give them
justice soon enough. But when the Son of
man comes, will he find faith on earth?'

Luke 18:1–8

The Pharisee and the tax-collector

Here is another parable that he told; it was aimed at those who were sure of their own goodness and looked down on everyone else. 'Two men went up to the temple to pray, one a Pharisee and the other a tax-collector. The Pharisee stood up and prayed this prayer: "I thank you, God, that I am not like the rest of mankind – greedy, dishonest, adulterous – or, for that matter, like this tax-collector. I fast twice a week; I pay tithes on all that I get." But the other kept his distance and would not even raise his eyes to heaven, but beat upon his breast, saying, "God, have mercy on me, sinner that I am." It was this man, I tell you, and not the other, who went home acquitted of his sins. For everyone who exalts himself will be humbled; and whoever humbles himself will be exalted.'

Luke 18:9–14

The Master and His Opponents

'THOSE WHO ARE WELL HAVE NO NEED OF A PHYSICIAN'

After this he went out and saw a tax-collector named Levi, sitting at the tax booth; and he said to him, 'Follow me.' And he got up, left everything, and followed him.

Then Levi gave a great banquet for him in his house; and there was a large crowd of tax-collectors and others sitting at the table with them. The Pharisees and their scribes were complaining to his disciples, saying, 'Why do you eat and drink with tax-collectors and sinners?' Jesus answered, 'Those who are well have no need of a physician, but those who are sick; I have come to call not the righteous but sinners to repentance.'

Luke 5:27–32

New wine in fresh wineskins

Then they said to him, 'John's disciples, like
the disciples of the Pharisees, frequently fast
and pray, but your disciples eat and drink.'
Jesus said to them, 'You cannot make
wedding-guests fast while the bridegroom is
with them, can you? The days will come
when the bridegroom will be taken away from
them, and then they will fast in those days.'
He also told them a parable: 'No one tears a
piece from a new garment and sews it on an
old garment; otherwise the new will be torn,
and the piece from the new will not match
the old. And no one puts new wine into old
wineskins; otherwise the new wine will burst
the skins and will be spilled, and the skins
will be destroyed. But new wine must be put
into fresh wineskins. And no one after
drinking old wine desires new wine, but says,
"The old is good."'

Luke 5:33–39

'Wisdom is vindicated by all her children'

'To what then will I compare the people of
this generation, and what are they like? They
are like children sitting in the market-place
and calling to one another,

> We played the flute for you,
>   and you did not dance;
> we wailed, and you did not weep.

For John the Baptist has come eating no
bread and drinking no wine, and you say,
"He has a demon"; the Son of man has
come eating and drinking, and you say,
"Look, a glutton and a drunkard, a friend
of tax-collectors and sinners!" Nevertheless,
wisdom is vindicated by all her children.'

Luke 7:31–35

'HER SINS, WHICH WERE MANY, HAVE BEEN FORGIVEN'

One of the Pharisees asked Jesus to eat with him, and he went into the Pharisee's house and took his place at the table. And a woman in the city, who was a sinner, having learned that he was eating in the Pharisee's house, brought an alabaster jar of ointment. She stood behind him at his feet, weeping, and began to bathe his feet with her tears and to dry them with her hair. Then she continued kissing his feet and anointing them with the ointment. Now when the Pharisee who had invited him saw it, he said to himself, 'If this man were a prophet, he would have known who and what kind of woman this is who is touching him – that she is a sinner.' Jesus spoke up and said to him, 'Simon, I have something to say to you.' 'Teacher,' he replied, 'speak.' 'A certain creditor had two debtors; one owed five hundred denarii, and the other fifty. When they could not pay, he cancelled the debts for both of them. Now which of them will love him more?' Simon answered, 'I suppose the one for whom he cancelled the greater debt.' And Jesus said to him, 'You have judged rightly.' Then turning towards the woman, he said to Simon, 'Do you see this woman? I entered your house; you gave me no water for my feet, but she has bathed my feet with her tears and dried them with her hair. You gave me no kiss, but from the time I came in she has not stopped kissing my feet. You did not anoint my head with oil, but she has anointed my feet with ointment. Therefore, I tell you, her sins, which were many, have been forgiven; hence she has shown great love. But the one to whom little is forgiven, loves little.' Then he said to her, 'Your sins are forgiven.' But those who were at the table with him began to say among themselves, 'Who is this who even forgives sins?' And he said to the woman, 'Your faith has saved you; go in peace.'

Luke 7:36–50

'THE SABBATH WAS MADE FOR HUMANKIND'

One sabbath he was going through the cornfields; and as they made their way his disciples began to pluck heads of grain. The Pharisees said to him, 'Look, why are they doing what is not lawful on the sabbath?' And he said to them, 'Have you never read what David did when he and his companions were hungry and in need of food? He entered the house of God, when Abiathar was high priest, and ate the bread of the Presence, which it is not lawful for any but the priests to eat, and he gave some to his companions.' Then he said to them, 'The sabbath was made for humankind, and not humankind for the sabbath; so the Son of man is lord even of the sabbath.'

Again he entered the synagogue, and a man was there who had a withered hand. They watched him to see whether he would cure him on the sabbath, so that they might accuse him. And he said to the man who had the withered hand, 'Come forward.' Then he said to them, 'Is it lawful to do good or to do harm on the sabbath, to save life or to kill?' But they were silent. He looked around at them with anger; he was grieved at their hardness of heart and said to the man, 'Stretch out your hand.' He stretched it out, and his hand was restored.

The Pharisees went out and immediately conspired with the Herodians against him, how to destroy him.

Mark 2:23 – 3:6

THE INTENTIONS OF THE HEART

Now when the Pharisees and some of the scribes who had come from Jerusalem gathered around him, they noticed that some of his disciples were eating with defiled hands, that is, without washing them. (For the Pharisees, and all the Jews, do not eat unless they thoroughly wash their hands, thus observing the tradition of the elders; and they do not eat anything from the market unless they wash it; and there are also many other traditions that they observe, the washing of cups, pots, and bronze kettles.) So the Pharisees and the scribes asked him, 'Why do your disciples not live according to the tradition of the elders, but eat with defiled hands?' He said to them, 'Isaiah prophesied rightly about you hypocrites, as it is written,

This people honours me with their lips,
but their hearts are far from me;
in vain do they worship me,
teaching human precepts as doctrines.

You abandon the commandment of God and hold to human tradition.'...

Then he called the crowd again and said to them, 'Listen to me, all of you, and understand: there is nothing outside a person that by going in can defile, but the things that come out are what defile... For it is from within, from the human heart, that evil intentions come: fornication, theft, murder, adultery, avarice, wickedness, deceit, licentiousness, envy, slander, pride, folly. All these evil things come from within, and they defile a person.'

Mark 7:1–8, 14–15, 21–23

98

'WHAT GOD HAS JOINED TOGETHER…'

Some Pharisees came, and to test him they asked, 'Is it lawful for a man to divorce his wife?' He answered them, 'What did Moses command you?' They said, 'Moses allowed a man to write a certificate of dismissal and to divorce her.' But Jesus said to them, 'Because of your hardness of heart he wrote this commandment for you. But from the beginning of creation, "God made them male and female." "For this reason a man shall leave his father and

mother and be joined to his wife, and the two shall become one flesh." So they are no longer two, but one flesh. Therefore what God has joined together, let no one separate.'

Then in the house the disciples asked him again about this matter. He said to them, 'Whoever divorces his wife and marries another commits adultery against her.'

Mark 10:2–11

A KINGDOM DIVIDED
AGAINST ITSELF

Then they brought to him a demoniac who was blind and mute; and he cured him, so that the one who had been mute could speak and see. All the crowds were amazed and said, 'Can this be the Son of David?' But when the Pharisees heard it, they said, 'It is only by Beelzebul, the ruler of the demons, that this fellow casts out the demons.' He knew what they were thinking and said to them, 'Every kingdom divided against itself is laid waste, and no city or house divided against itself will stand. If Satan casts out Satan, he is divided against himself; how then will his kingdom stand? If I cast out demons by Beelzebul, by whom do your own exorcists cast them out? Therefore they will be your judges. But if it is by the Spirit of God that I cast out demons, then the kingdom of God has come to you. Or how can one enter a strong man's house and plunder his property, without first tying up the strong man? Then indeed the house can be plundered.'

Matthew 12:22–29

THE UNFORGIVABLE SIN

'Whoever is not with me is against me, and
whoever does not gather with me scatters.
Therefore I tell you, people will be forgiven
for every sin and blasphemy, but blasphemy
against the Spirit will not be forgiven.
Whoever speaks a word against the Son of
man will be forgiven, but whoever speaks
against the Holy Spirit will not be forgiven,
either in this age or in the age to come.'

Matthew 12:30–32

'EVERY CARELESS WORD'

'You brood of vipers! How can you speak good things, when you are evil? For out of the abundance of the heart the mouth speaks. The good person brings good things out of a good treasure, and the evil person brings evil things out of an evil treasure. I tell you, on the day of judgment you will have to give an account for every careless word you utter; for by your words you will be justified, and by your words you will be condemned.'

Matthew 12:34–37

AN EVIL GENERATION

Then some of the scribes and Pharisees said to him, 'Teacher, we wish to see a sign from you.' But he answered them, 'An evil and adulterous generation asks for a sign, but no sign will be given to it except the sign of the prophet Jonah. For just as Jonah was for three days and three nights in the belly of the sea monster, so for three days and three nights the Son of man will be in the heart of the earth. The people of Nineveh will rise up at the judgment with this generation and condemn it, because they repented at the proclamation of Jonah, and see, something greater than Jonah is here! The queen of the South will rise up at the judgment with this generation and condemn it, because she came from the ends of the earth to listen to the wisdom of Solomon, and see, something greater than Solomon is here!'

Matthew 12:38–42

A RESTLESS SPIRIT

'When the unclean spirit
has gone out of a person, it
wanders through waterless
regions looking for a
resting-place, but it finds
none. Then it says, "I will
return to my house from
which I came." When it
comes, it finds it empty,
swept, and put in order.
Then it goes and brings
along seven other spirits
more evil than itself, and
they enter and live there;
and the last state of that
person is worse than the
first. So will it be also with
this evil generation.'

Matthew 12:43–45

'YOU CANNOT SERVE GOD AND WEALTH'

'No slave can serve two masters; for a slave
will either hate the one and love the other,
or be devoted to the one and despise the
other. You cannot serve God and wealth.'

The Pharisees, who were lovers of
money, heard all this, and they ridiculed him.
So he said to them, 'You are those who
justify yourselves in the sight of others; but
God knows your hearts; for what is prized
by human beings is an abomination in the
sight of God.'

Luke 16:13–15

Signs of the times

The Pharisees and Sadducees came, and to test Jesus they asked him to show them a sign from heaven. He answered them, 'When it is evening, you say, "It will be fair weather, for the sky is red." And in the morning, "It will be stormy today, for the sky is red and threatening." You know how to interpret the appearance of the sky, but you cannot interpret the signs of the times.'

Matthew 16:1–3

The two sons

'What do you think? A man had two sons; he went to the first and said, "Son, go and work in the vineyard today." He answered, "I will not"; but later he changed his mind and went. The father went to the second and said the same; and he answered, "I go, sir"; but he did not go. Which of the two did the will of his father?' They said, 'The first.' Jesus said to them, 'Truly I tell you, the tax-collectors and the prostitutes are going into the kingdom of God ahead of you. For John came to you in the way of righteousness and you did not believe him, but the tax-collectors and the prostitutes believed him; and even after you saw it, you did not change your minds and believe him.'

Matthew 21:28–32

'GIVE TO THE EMPEROR THE THINGS THAT ARE THE EMPEROR'S'

Then they sent to him some Pharisees and some Herodians to trap him in what he said. And they came and said to him, 'Teacher, we know that you are sincere, and show deference to no one; for you do not regard people with partiality, but teach the way of God in accordance with truth. Is it lawful to pay taxes to the emperor, or not? Should we pay them, or should we not?' But knowing their hypocrisy, he said to them, 'Why are you putting me to the test? Bring me a denarius and let me see it.' And they brought one. Then he said to them, 'Whose head is this, and whose title?' They answered, 'The emperor's.' Jesus said to them, 'Give to the emperor the things that are the emperor's, and to God the things that are God's.' And they were utterly amazed at him.

Mark 12:13–17

THE GOD OF THE LIVING

Some Sadducees, who say there is no resurrection, came to him and asked him a question, saying, 'Teacher, Moses wrote for us that if a man's brother dies, leaving a wife but no child, the man shall marry the widow and raise up children for his brother. There were seven brothers; the first married and, when he died, left no children; and the second married her and died, leaving no children; and the third likewise; none of the seven left children. Last of all the woman herself died. In the resurrection whose wife will she be? For the seven had married her.'

Jesus said to them, 'Is not this the reason you are wrong, that you know neither the scriptures nor the power of God? For when they rise from the dead, they neither marry nor are given in marriage, but are like angels in heaven. And as for the dead being raised, have you not read in the book of Moses, in the story about the bush, how God said to him, "I am the God of Abraham, the God of Isaac, and the God of Jacob"? He is God not of the dead, but of the living; you are quite wrong.'

Mark 12:18–27

THE TWO GREAT COMMANDMENTS

One of the scribes came near and heard them disputing with one another, and seeing that he answered them well, he asked him, 'Which commandment is the first of all?' Jesus answered, 'The first is, "Hear, O Israel: the Lord our God, the Lord is one; you shall love the Lord your God with all your heart, and with all your soul, and with all your mind, and with all your strength." The second is this, "You shall love your neighbour as yourself." There is no other commandment greater than these.' Then the scribe said to him, 'You are right, Teacher; you have truly said that "he is one, and besides him there is no other"; and "to love him with all the heart, and with all the understanding, and with all the strength", and "to love one's neighbour as oneself" — this is much more important than all whole burnt-offerings and sacrifices.' When Jesus saw that he answered wisely, he said to him, 'You are not far from the kingdom of God.' After that no one dared to ask him any question.

Mark 12:28–34

'Woe to you, scribes and Pharisees'

Then Jesus said to the crowds and to his disciples, 'The scribes and the Pharisees sit on Moses' seat; therefore, do whatever they teach you and follow it; but do not do as they do, for they do not practise what they teach. They tie up heavy burdens, hard to bear, and lay them on the shoulders of others; but they themselves are unwilling to lift a finger to move them. They do all their deeds to be seen by others; for they make their phylacteries broad and their fringes long. They love to have the place of honour at banquets and the best seats in the synagogues, and to be greeted with respect in the market-places, and to have people call them rabbi. But you are not to be called rabbi, for you have one teacher, and you are all students. And call no one your father on earth, for you have one Father – the one in heaven. Nor are you to be called instructors, for you have one instructor, the Messiah. The greatest among you will be your servant. All who exalt themselves will be humbled, and all who humble themselves will be exalted.

'But woe to you, scribes and Pharisees, hypocrites! For you lock people out of the kingdom of heaven. For you do not go in yourselves, and when others are going in, you stop them…

'Woe to you, scribes and Pharisees, hypocrites! For you tithe mint, dill, and cummin, and have neglected the weightier matters of the law: justice and mercy and faith. It is these you ought to have practised without neglecting the others. You blind guides! You strain out a gnat but swallow a camel!

'Woe to you, scribes and Pharisees, hypocrites! For you clean the outside of the cup and of the plate, but inside they are full of greed and self-indulgence. You blind Pharisee! First clean the inside of the cup, so that the outside also may become clean…

'Jerusalem, Jerusalem, the city that kills the prophets and stones those who are sent to it! How often have I desired to gather your children together as a hen gathers her brood under her wings, and you were not willing! See, your house is left to you, desolate. For I tell you, you will not see me again until you say, "Blessed is the one who comes in the name of the Lord."'

Matthew 23:1–13, 23–26, 37–39

The·Darkness Defeated

THE RESURRECTION AND THE LIFE

There was a man named Lazarus of Bethany, the village of Mary and her sister, Martha, and he was ill…

Jesus loved Martha and her sister and Lazarus, yet when he heard that he was ill he stayed where he was for two more days before saying to the disciples, 'Let us go back to Judea.'…

He said that and then added, 'Our friend Lazarus is at rest; I am going to wake him.' The disciples said to him, 'Lord, if he is at rest he will be saved.' Jesus was speaking of the death of Lazarus, but they thought that by 'rest' he meant 'sleep'…

On arriving, Jesus found that Lazarus had been in the tomb for four days already. Bethany is only about two miles from Jerusalem, and many Jews had come to Martha and Mary to comfort them about their brother. When Martha heard that Jesus was coming she went to meet him. Mary remained sitting in the house. Martha said to Jesus, 'Lord, if you had been here, my brother would not have died, but even now I know that God will grant whatever you ask of him.' Jesus said to her, 'Your brother will rise again.' Martha said, 'I know he will rise again at the resurrection on the last day.' Jesus said:

I am the resurrection.
Anyone who believes in me,
    even though that person dies, will live,
and whoever lives and believes in me
will never die.
Do you believe this?

'Yes, Lord,' she said, 'I believe that you are the Christ, the Son of God, the one who was to come into this world.'

When she had said this, she went and called her sister Mary, saying in a low voice, 'The Master is here and wants to see you.'…

At the sight of her tears, and those of the Jews who had come with her, Jesus was greatly distressed, and with a profound sigh he said, 'Where have you put him?' They said, 'Lord, come and see.' Jesus wept; and the Jews said,

'See how much he loved him!'…

Sighing again, Jesus reached the tomb: it was a cave with a stone to close the opening. Jesus said, 'Take the stone away.'…

So they took the stone away. Then Jesus lifted up his eyes and said:

Father, I thank you
*   for hearing my prayer.*
I myself knew that you hear me always,
but I speak
for the sake of all these
*   who are standing around me,*
so that they may believe
*   it was you who sent me.*

When he had said this, he cried in a loud voice, 'Lazarus, come out!' The dead man came out, his feet and hands bound with strips of material, and a cloth over his face. Jesus said to them, 'Unbind him, let him go free.'

John 11:1, 5–7, 11–13, 17–28, 33–36, 38–39, 41–44

Mary anoints her Master's feet

Six days before the Passover, Jesus went to Bethany, where Lazarus was, whom he had raised from the dead. They gave a dinner for him there; Martha waited on them and Lazarus was among those at table. Mary brought in a pound of very costly ointment, pure nard, and with it anointed the feet of Jesus, wiping them with her hair; the house was filled with the scent of the ointment. Then Judas Iscariot – one of his disciples, the man who was to betray him – said, 'Why was this ointment not sold for three hundred denarii and the money given to the poor?' He said this, not because he cared about the poor, but

because he was a thief; he was in charge of the common fund and used to help himself to the contents. So Jesus said, 'Leave her alone; let her keep it for the day of my burial. You have the poor with you always, you will not always have me.'

John 12:1–8

THE GRAIN OF WHEAT

Among those who went up to worship at the
festival were some Greeks. These
approached Philip, who came
from Bethsaida in Galilee, and
put this request to him, 'Sir, we
should like to see Jesus.' Philip
went to tell Andrew, and Andrew
and Philip together went to
tell Jesus.

    Jesus replied to them:

Now the hour has come
for the Son of man to be glorified.
In all truth I tell you,
unless a wheat grain falls into the earth
    and dies,
it remains only a single grain;
but if it dies
it yields a rich harvest.
Anyone who loves his life loses it;
anyone who hates his life in this world
will keep it for eternal life.
Whoever serves me, must follow me,
and my servant will be with me
    wherever I am.
If anyone serves me,
    my Father will honour him.

John 12:20–26

THE JUDGMENT

'Whoever believes in me
believes not in me
but in the one
 who sent me,
and whoever sees me,
sees the one who sent me.
I have come into the
 world as light,
to prevent anyone
 who believes in me
from staying in the dark
 any more.

If anyone hears my words
    and does not keep them faithfully,
it is not I who shall judge such a person,
since I have come not to judge the world,
but to save the world:
anyone who rejects me
    and refuses my words
has his judge already:
the word itself that I have spoken
will be his judge on the last day.'

John 12:44–48

THE MASTER WASHES HIS DISCIPLES' FEET

Before the festival of the Passover, Jesus,
knowing that his hour had come to pass
from this world to the Father, having loved
those who were his in the world, loved them
to the end.

They were at supper, and the devil had
already put it into the mind of Judas Iscariot
son of Simon, to betray him. Jesus knew
that the Father had put everything into his
hands, and that he had come from God and
was returning to God, and he got up from
table, removed his outer garments and,
taking a towel, wrapped it round his waist;
he then poured water into a basin and began

to wash the disciples' feet and to wipe them with the towel he was wearing.

He came to Simon Peter, who said to him, 'Lord, are you going to wash my feet?' Jesus answered, 'At the

moment you do not know what I am doing, but later you will understand.' 'Never!' said Peter. 'You shall never wash my feet.' Jesus replied, 'If I do not wash you, you can have no share with me.' Simon Peter said, 'Well then, Lord, not only my feet, but my hands and my head as well!' Jesus said, 'No one who has had a bath needs washing, such a person is clean all over. You too are clean, though not all of you are.' He knew who was going to betray him, and that was why he said, 'though not all of you are'.

When he had washed their feet and put on his outer garments again he went back to the table. 'Do you understand', he said, 'what I have done to you? You call me Master and Lord, and rightly; so I am. If I, then, the Lord and Master, have washed your feet, you must wash each other's feet. I have given you an example so that you may copy what I have done to you.

In all truth I tell you,
no servant is greater than his master,
no messenger is greater
than the one who sent him.

'Now that you know this, blessed are you if you behave accordingly.'

John 13:1–17

'Love one another'

*'I give you a new commandment:
love one another;
you must love one another
just as I have loved you.
It is by your love for one another,
that everyone will recognize you
as my disciples.'*

John 13:34–35

The Way, Truth and Life

*'Do not let your hearts be troubled.
You trust in God, trust also in me.
In my Father's house
    there are many places to live in;
otherwise I would have told you.
I am going now to prepare a place for you,
and after I have gone
    and prepared you a place,
I shall return to take you to myself,
so that you may be with me
where I am.
You know the way
    to the place where I am going.'*

Thomas said, 'Lord, we do not know where
you are going, so how can we know the way?'
Jesus said:

> I am the Way; I am Truth and Life.
> No one can come to the Father
>   except through me.
> If you know me,
>   you will know my Father too.
> From this moment you know him
>   and have seen him.

Philip said, 'Lord, show us the Father and
then we shall be satisfied.' Jesus said to him,
'Have I been with you all this time, Philip,
and you still do not know me?

> Anyone who has seen me
> has seen the Father.'

John 14:1–9

> 'I shall not leave you orphans;
> I shall come to you.
> In a short time
>   the world will no longer see me;
> but you will see that I live
> and you also will live.
> On that day
> you will know that I am in my Father
> and you in me and I in you.
> Whoever holds to my commandments
>   and keeps them
> is the one who loves me;
> and whoever loves me
>   will be loved by my Father,
> and I shall love him
>   and reveal myself to him.'

Judas – not Judas Iscariot – said to him,
'Lord, what has happened, that you intend to
show yourself to us and not to the world?'
Jesus replied:

> Anyone who loves me will keep my word,
> and my Father will love him,
> and we shall come to him
> and make a home in him.

Anyone who does not love me
　　does not keep my words.
And the word that you hear
　　is not my own:
it is the word of the Father who sent me.
I have said these things to you
while still with you;
but the Paraclete, the Holy Spirit,
whom the Father will send in my name,
will teach you everything
and remind you of all I have said to you.
Peace I bequeath to you,
my own peace I give you,
a peace which the world cannot give,
　　this is my gift to you.
Do not let your hearts be troubled
　　or afraid.

　　　　John 14:18–27

THE TRUE VINE

'I am the true vine,
and my Father is the vinedresser.
Every branch in me that bears no fruit
he cuts away,
and every branch that does bear fruit he prunes
to make it bear even more.
You are clean already,
by means of the word
    that I have spoken to you.
Remain in me, as I in you.
As a branch cannot bear fruit all by itself,
unless it remains part of the vine,
neither can you unless you remain in me.
I am the vine,
you are the branches.
Whoever remains in me, with me in him,
bears fruit in plenty;
for cut off from me you can do nothing.
Anyone who does not remain in me
is thrown away like a branch
— and withers;
these branches are collected
    and thrown on the fire
and are burnt.
If you remain in me
and my words remain in you,
you may ask for whatever you please
and you will get it.
It is to the glory of my Father
    that you should bear much fruit
and be my disciples.'
        John 15:1–8

THE GREATEST LOVE

'I have loved you
just as the Father has loved me.
Remain in my love.
If you keep my commandments
you will remain in my love,
just as I have kept
    my Father's commandments
and remain in his love.
I have told you this
so that my own joy may be in you
and your joy be complete.
This is my commandment:
love one another,
as I have loved you.
No one can have greater love
than to lay down his life for his friends.'
        John 15:9–13

THE SPIRIT OF TRUTH

'I still have many things to say to you
but they would be too much for you
*   to bear now.*
However, when the Spirit of truth comes
he will lead you to the complete truth,
since he will not be speaking
*   of his own accord,*
but will say only what he has been told;
and he will reveal to you
*   the things to come.*
He will glorify me,
since all he reveals to you
will be taken from what is mine.
Everything the Father has is mine;
that is why I said:
all he reveals to you
will be taken from what is mine...
I have told you all this
so that you may find peace in me.
In the world you will have hardship,
but be courageous:
I have conquered the world.'

John 16:12–15, 33

Picture Acknowledgments

52: *Descent into the Empyrean* (detail), by Hieronymus Bosch (c.1450–1516): Palazzo Ducale, Venice/Bridgeman Art Library, London/New York.

55: *Christ in the Wilderness*, by Briton Rivière (1840–1920): Guildhall Art Gallery, Corporation of London/Bridgeman Art Library, London/New York.

57: *Woman with a Candle*, by Godfried Schalken or Schalcken (1643–1706): Palazzo Pitti, Florence/Bridgeman Art Library, London/New York.

58: *The Sower*, from *The Life of Christ by an Indian Artist*, courtesy of The United Society for the Propagation of the Gospel.

61: *The Miraculous Catch*, from *The Life of Christ by Chinese Artists*, courtesy of The United Society for the Propagation of the Gospel.

61: *Shimadai and Ainame*, from the series 'The Large Fish', Utagawa School, c.1840–42 (woodblock hand-coloured print on paper), by Ando or Utagawa Hiroshige (1797–1858): Johannesburg Art Gallery/Bridgeman Art Library, London/New York.

62: f.20v *Astrological sign: Libra* (detail), 16th century, Turkish (literary text): Bibliothèque Nationale, Paris/Bridgeman Art Library, London/New York.

63: *Parable of the Blind*, 1568, by Pieter the Elder Brueghel (c.1515–69): Museo e Gallerie Nazionali di Capodimonte, Naples/Bridgeman Art Library, London/New York.

65: *Jerusalem, Jerusalem*, illustration for *The Life of Christ*, c.1886–96 (gouache on paperboard), by James Jacques Joseph Tissot (1836–1902): Brooklyn Museum of Art, New York/Bridgeman Art Library, London/New York.

66–67: *January: Banquet Scene*, by the Limbourg brothers (detail) (facsimile manuscript), from the *Très Riches Heures du Duc de Berry* (early 15th century): Victoria & Albert Museum, London/Bridgeman Art Library, London/New York.

68: *September: Harvesting Grapes*, by the Limbourg brothers (facsimile manuscript), from the *Très Riches Heures du Duc de Berry* (early 15th century): Victoria & Albert Museum, London/Bridgeman Art Library, London/New York.

70: *Wheat Field with Sheaves*, 1888, by Vincent van Gogh (1853–90): Israel Museum, Jerusalem/Bridgeman Art Library, London/New York.

73: *The Table of the Seven Deadly Sins*, by Hieronymus Bosch (detail) (c.1450–1516): Prado, Madrid/Bridgeman Art Library, London/New York.

74: *The Parable of the Labourers in the Vineyard*, by Rembrandt Harmensz van Rijn (1606–69): Hermitage, St Petersburg/Bridgeman Art Library, London/New York.

75: *The Vinedressers Killing the Heir of the Vineyard Owner, Illustrating Christ's Teaching, 'The Stone that the Builders Rejected is the Chief Stone of the Corner'* (detail), section of wing panel, from the Mompelgarter Altarpiece (panel), by Matthias Gerung or Gerou (c.1500–68/70): Kunsthistorisches Museum, Vienna/Bridgeman Art Library, London/New York.

76: *The Five Wise and Five Foolish Virgins*, by Peter von Cornelius: Yale University, New Haven, C.T./SuperStock.

77: *The Slothful Servant Burying his Money, from the Parable of the Talents*, Flemish, 17th century (stained glass): Church of St Mary, Addington/Bridgeman Art Library, London/New York.

79: *Christ Separates the Sheep from the Goats*, 6th century (mosaic): San Apollinare Nuovo, Ravenna/Bridgeman Art Library, London/New York.

80: *The Good Samaritan*, from *The Life of Christ by an Indian Artist*, courtesy of The United Society for the Propagation of the Gospel.

81: *Month of September: Parable of the Rich Man who Built Greater Barns*, by Abel Grimmer or Grimer (1570–1619): Christie's Images/Bridgeman Art Library, London/New York.

82: *Gluttony and Abstinence* (detail), by Jacques le Grant, *Book of Good Morals* (15th century): Musée Condé, Chantilly/Bridgeman Art Library, London/New York.

84: Ms 439 f.9r *Banquet Scene with Men Drinking Coffee, Guests of Honour Sitting in a Recess, Entertained by Three Musicians, while an Old Man is Taken Ill*, from an album of painting and calligraphy, Turkish, c.16th–17th century: Chester Beatty Library and Gallery of Oriental Art, Dublin/Bridgeman Art Library, London/New York.

87: *The Prodigal Son*, by Pierre Puvis de Chavannes: National Gallery of Art, Washington, D.C./SuperStock.

90: *Lazarus and the Rich Man's Table (Luke 16)* (detail), section of wing panel, from the Mompelgarter Altarpiece (panel), by Matthias Gerung or Gerou (c.1500–68/70):

Kunsthistorisches Museum, Vienna/Bridgeman Art Library, London/New York.

93: *Jesus Taken up to a Pinnacle of the Temple*, by James Jacques Tissot: SuperStock.

96: *Mary Bathing Christ's Feet*, from *The Life of Christ by an Indian Artist*, courtesy of The United Society for the Propagation of the Gospel.

97: *August: Pharisees Censuring Christ for Permitting his Disciples to Eat on the Sabbath*, by Abel Grimmer or Grimer (1570–1619): Christie's Images, London/Bridgeman Art Library, London/New York.

99: *Nuptial Couple against a Green Background*, by Marc Chagall (1887–1985): Christie's Images, London/Bridgeman Art Library, London/New York. © ADAGP, Paris and DACS, London, 1999.

100: *Christ is Tempted to Turn Stones into Bread*, MS Gough liturg.2, f.22r: The Bodleian Library, University of Oxford.

101: *Gonzaga Family in Adoration* (detail), by Peter Paul Rubens: Palazzo Ducale, Mantua, Italy/SuperStock.

103: *Demons Armed with Sticks*, detail from the reverse of the Isenheim Altarpiece, by Matthias Grünewald (Mathis Nithart Gothart) (c.1480–1528): Musée d'Unterlinden, Colmar/Bridgeman Art Library, London/New York.

105: Ms 5064 f.68v *Hoeing and Pruning the Vines* (detail), by the Master of the Workshop of Margaret of York, Bruges, Rustican (15th century): Bibliothèque Nationale, Paris/Bridgeman Art Library, London/New York.

106: *The Marriage of the Virgin*, detail of the high priest, 1500–4 (oil on canvas), by Pietro Perugino (c.1445–1523): Musée des Beaux Arts, Caen/Peter Willi/Bridgeman Art Library, London/New York.

109: Jewish rug, depicting the Dome of the Rock and Tombs of Absalom and Zachariah, made by the Bezalel workshop in Jerusalem, c.1920 (cotton and wool): Private Collection/Bridgeman Art Library, London/New York.

111: *Maestà: Descent into Limbo* (detail), 1308–11, by Duccio di Buoninsegna (c.1278–1318): Museo dell'Opera del Duomo, Siena/Bridgeman Art Library, London/New York.

112–13: *The Raising of Lazarus*, c.1305 (fresco), by Giotto di Bondone (c.1266–1337): Scrovegni (Arena) Chapel, Padua/Bridgeman Art Library, London/New York.

114: *Jesus and Mary Magdalene*, Chinese painting of silk: Sonia Halliday Photographs/Laura Lushington.

116: *St Michael Weighing Souls at the Last Judgment*, by Rogier van der Weyden (1399–1464): Hotel Dieu, Beaune/Bridgeman Art Library, London/New York.

118: *Christ Washing the Disciples' Feet*, School of Arezzo: SuperStock.

119: *The Annunciation to the Shepherds*, detail of the angel, 1656, by Nicolaes Pietersz Berchem (1620–83): City of Bristol Museum and Art Gallery/Bridgeman Art Library, London/New York.

121: *Sacré-Cœur Crucifié (The Crucifixion)*, c.1894, by Maurice Denis: Private Collection/Giraudon, Paris/SuperStock. © ADAGP, Paris and DACS, London, 1999.

123: *The Resurrection*, by Matthias Grünewald: SuperStock.

125: *St Matthew the Evangelist*, by Giusto di Giovanni Menabuoi: Baptistry of the Cathedral, Padua, Italy/SuperStock.

All other illustrations from Dover Pictorial Archive Series.